a collection of
CHARACTERS

4 Knit Toys with Matching Blankets

Add a little character to your décor! These four blanket-and-animal sets were designed with both beauty and fun in mind. Designer Chris de Longpré used her knitting wizardry to create four whimsical characters that are the perfect complement to their matching blankets. You can knit a duck, dog, pig, or mouse to brighten each room of your house. And each animal or blanket would also make a thoughtful gift, all by itself.

about Chris de Longpé

"For me, designing is a very personal experience," says Chris de Longpré. "When I finish a design, I feel strongly connected to it."

The Michigan resident is even more fond of her four grandchildren. In fact, she is quick to say that her family is the greatest love of her life. Husband John and daughters Gini and Elli all pitch in to help Chris with her design business, Knitting at KNoon.

"When my daughters started their families," Chris says, "I found that designing and knitting for the babies was a wonderful creative outlet. At the urging of my local yarn shop owner, I wrote up a few patterns for sale in her shop. Those early successes led to the formation of Knitting At KNoon Designs, LLC, the pattern publishing company I started in 2003."

Chris explains the unusual name: "Before I retired to work full-time at designing, I worked at a local hospital in information services. During lunch, I taught knitting to my colleagues. We called those classes Knitting at KNoon. I started writing patterns for the classes, and the business just grew out of what I was doing on a volunteer basis. It became so much more fun than my real job that I decided to make it my real job."

To see more of Chris's imaginative designs, visit her Web site at www.KnittingAtKNoon.com. While you're online, drop by www.leisurearts. com to find a wide variety of knitting books on everything from afghans to wearables.

LEISURE ARTS, INC
Little Rock, Arkansas

snips and snails
PUPPY DOG TAILS

WOOF the PUPPY

 INTERMEDIATE

Finished Size: 7" (18 cm) tall (seated)

MATERIALS
Medium Weight Yarn 4
   White - 60 yards (55 meters)
   Blue Tweed - 30 yards (27.5 meters)
   Blue - small amount
Double pointed knitting needles, size 6 (4 mm)
   (set of 4) **or** size needed for gauge
Split ring marker
Polyester fiberfill
Yarn needle

GAUGE: In Stockinette Stitch,
          18 sts and 24 rows = 4" (10 cm)

Instructions begin on page 4.

🐰 BODY

With White, cast 6 sts onto a double pointed needle; transfer 2 sts onto each of two other needles *(see Knitting in the Round, page 28)*.

Place a split ring marker around first cast on stitch to mark beginning of round *(see Markers, page 28)*. Begin working in rounds, making sure that first round is not twisted.

Rnd 1: Knit around.

Rnd 2: Knit increase in each st around *(Figs. 6a & b, page 29)*: 12 sts.

Rnds 3 and 4: Repeat Rnds 1 and 2: 24 sts.

Rnds 5 and 6: Knit around.

Rnd 7: (K1, knit increase) around: 36 sts.

Rnds 8-10: Knit around.

Rnd 11: (K2, knit increase) around: 48 sts.

Rnds 12-18: Knit around.

Rnd 19 (Decrease rnd): ★ K2, SSK *(Figs. 11a-c, page 30)*, knit across to last 4 sts on needle, K2 tog *(Fig. 10, page 29)*, K2; repeat from ★ across each needle: 42 sts.

Rnds 20-23: Knit around.

Rnd 24: Repeat Rnd 19: 36 sts.

Rnds 25-29: Knit around.

Rnd 30: Repeat Rnd 19: 30 sts.

Rnds 31-33: Knit around.

Rnd 34: Repeat Rnd 19: 24 sts.

Leaving sts on needles, lightly stuff Body.

Rnd 35: K2 tog around: 12 sts.

🐰 BACK NECK

Redistribute sts onto two needles, 6 sts each, with **wrong** side facing and working yarn on right hand end of one needle. Remove marker and begin working in rows.

Row 1: Purl increase in each st across first needle **only** *(Fig. 9, page 29)*, leave remaining 6 sts on hold: 12 sts.

Row 2: Slip 1 as if to **purl**, knit across.

Row 3: Slip 1 as if to **purl**, purl across.

Rows 4-12: Repeat Rows 2 and 3, 4 times; then repeat Row 2 once **more**.

HEAD
CROWN SHAPING
Row 1: Slip 1 as if to **purl**, P5, P2 tog **(Fig. 14, page 30)**, P1, leave remaining 3 sts unworked.

Row 2: Turn; slip 1 as if to **purl**, K1, K2 tog, K1, leave remaining 3 sts unworked.

Row 3: Turn; slip 1 as if to **purl**, P2, P2 tog, P1, leave last st unworked.

Row 4: Turn; slip 1 as if to **purl**, K3, K2 tog, K1, leave last st unworked.

Row 5: Turn; slip 1 as if to **purl**, P3, P2 tog, P1.

Row 6: K5, K2 tog: 6 sts.

FACE
With same needle holding Crown sts, pick up 7 sts along first neck edge **(Fig. 16a, page 31)**. With an empty needle, knit across 6 front neck sts. With an empty needle, pick up 7 sts along second neck edge, then knit first 3 sts from first needle. Place split ring marker around first st to mark beginning of rnd. There will be 10 sts on first needle, 6 sts on second needle, and 10 sts on third needle, 26 sts total.

Rnd 1: Knit around.

Rnd 2 (Decrease rnd)**:** Knit across to last 3 sts on first needle, K2 tog, K1; knit across 6 sts on second needle; K1, SSK, knit across on third needle: 24 sts.

Rnds 3-9: Repeat Rnds 1 and 2, 3 times; then repeat Rnd 1 once **more**: 18 sts.

Leaving sts on needles, lightly stuff Head.

Rnd 10: K2 tog around: 9 sts.

Cut yarn, leaving a long end.

Thread yarn needle with long end and weave through remaining sts, pull **tightly** and secure end.

MUZZLE
With Blue Tweed, cast 15 sts onto a double pointed needle; transfer 5 sts onto each of two other needles and place split ring marker around first st to mark beginning of rnd.

Rnds 1-4: Knit around.

Rnd 5: (K2 tog, K1, SSK) 3 times: 9 sts.

Rnd 6: Knit around.

Cut yarn, leaving a long end for sewing.

Thread yarn needle with long end and weave through remaining sts, pulling **tightly** to secure.

EAR (Make 2)
Ears are worked flat with two double pointed needles.

With Blue Tweed, cast on 19 sts.

Row 1 (Right side)**:** K8, (slip 2, K1, P2SSO **(Figs. 13a & b, page 30))**, K8: 17 sts.

Row 2: K8, P1, K8.

Row 3: K7, slip 2, K1, P2SSO, K7: 15 sts.

Row 4: K7, P1, K7.

Row 5: K6, slip 2, K1, P2SSO, K6: 13 sts.

Row 6: K6, P1, K6.

Row 7: K5, slip 2, K1, P2SSO, K5: 11 sts.

Row 8: K5, P1, K5.

Row 9: K4, slip 2, K1, P2SSO, K4: 9 sts.

Row 10: K4, P1, K4.

Row 11: K3, slip 2, K1, P2SSO, K3: 7 sts.

Instructions continued on page 6.

Row 12: K3, P1, K3.

Row 13: K2, slip 2, K1, P2SSO, K2: 5 sts.

Row 14: K2, P1, K2.

Row 15: K1, slip 2, K1, P2SSO, K1: 3 sts.

Row 16: K1, P1, K1.

Row 17: Slip 2, K1, P2SSO: one st.

Cut yarn and pull through last stitch.

TAIL

With Blue Tweed, cast 6 sts onto double pointed needle; transfer 2 sts onto each of two other needles. Place split ring marker around first st to mark beginning of rnd.

Rnds 1-6: Knit around.

Rnd 7: Knit all the sts onto working needle as follows: K2 tog, K2, SSK: 4 sts.

Remove marker and begin working in I-cord rows.

Row 1: Slide sts to opposite end of needle, K4.

Row 2: Slide sts to opposite end of needle, K1, K2 tog, K1: 3 sts.

Row: Slide sts to opposite end of needle, K3.

Bind off all sts in **knit**.

LEG (Make 4)

With White, cast 9 sts onto double pointed needle; transfer 3 sts onto each of two other needles. Place split ring marker around first st to mark beginning of rnd.

Rnds 1-20: Knit around; at end of Rnd 20, cut White.

FOOT

Rnd 1: With Blue Tweed, knit around.

Rnd 2: K2, knit increase 5 times, K2: 14 sts.

Rnds 3-5: Knit around.

Rnd 6: K2, K2 tog 5 times, K2: 9 sts.

Rnd 7: Knit around.

Rnd 8: K1, K2 tog 4 times: 5 sts.

Cut yarn, leaving a long end for sewing.

Stuff the Foot and the last 5 rnds of the Leg, leaving the rest of the Leg unstuffed.

Thread yarn needle with long end and weave through remaining sts, pull **tightly** and secure end.

FINISHING

Using photo as a guide for placement:
 Lightly stuff Muzzle and sew slightly above center of Face.
 Sew Legs to Body.
 Sew Tail to back at base of Body.
 Sew each Ear to top of Head, sewing ends of last 3 rows of Ear down to Head.
 With Blue, work satin stitch for the nose *(Fig. 19, page 31)* and French knots for the eyes *(Fig. 18, page 31)*. ❖

6

blanket

 EASY

 Finished Size: 30" x 40" (76 cm x 101.5 cm)

 MATERIALS
Medium Weight Yarn
   (3¹/₂ ounces, 196 yards
   (100 grams, 179 meters) per skein):
      7 skeins
32" (81.5 cm) Circular knitting needle, size 10
   (6 mm) **or** size needed for gauge
Crochet hook, size N (9 mm) (for fringe)

 GAUGE: In pattern, 20 sts = 4¹/₂" (11.5 cm);
                22 rows = 4" (10 cm)

 BODY
Cast on 134 sts.

Row 1: (Right side): P3, (slip 1 as if to **knit**, K2,
PSSO *(Fig. 12, page 30))*, ★ P2, slip 1 as if to
knit, K2, PSSO; repeat from ★ across to last
3 sts, P3: 108 sts.

Row 2: K3, P1, YO *(Fig. 17b, page 31)*, P1, (K2,
P1, YO, P1) across to last 3 sts, K3: 134 sts.

Row 3: P3, K3, (P2, K3) across to last 3 sts, P3.

Row 4: K3, P3, (K2, P3) across to last 3 sts, K3.

Rows 5-218: Repeat Rows 1-4, 53 times; then
repeat Rows 1 and 2 once **more**.

Bind off all sts in pattern.

 **FRINGE**
Cut a piece of cardboard 3" (7.5 cm) wide
and 8¹/₂" (21.5 cm) long. Wind the yarn
loosely and **evenly** lengthwise around the
cardboard until the card is filled, then cut
across one end; repeat as needed.

Hold two strands of yarn together; fold in
half.

With **wrong** side facing and using a crochet
hook, draw the folded end up through a
stitch and pull the loose ends through the
folded end *(Fig. 1a)*; draw the knot up **tightly**
(Fig. 1b). Repeat, spacing as desired.

Lay Blanket flat on a hard surface and trim
the ends. ❖

Fig. 1a	Fig. 1b

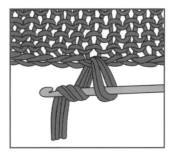 

the mouse
TAKES THE CHEESE

· ·

squeak
the
mouse

 INTERMEDIATE

Finished Size: 6" (15 cm) tall (seated, excluding ears)

MATERIALS
Bulky Weight Yarn 🔵5
    Blue - 65 yards (59.5 meters)
    Yellow - small amount
Double pointed knitting needles, size 5
    (3.75 mm) (set of 4) **or** size needed for gauge
Split ring marker
Polyester fiberfill
Yarn needle

GAUGE: In Stockinette Stitch,
        18 sts and 24 rows = 4" (10 cm)

Instructions begin on page 10.

Rnds 12 and 13: Knit around.

Rnd 14 (Decrease rnd):
★ K2, SSK *(Figs. 11a-c, page 30)*, knit across to last 4 sts on needle, K2 tog *(Fig. 10, page 29)*, K2; repeat from ★ across each needle: 42 sts.

Rnds 15-19: Knit around.

Rnd 20: Repeat Rnd 14: 36 sts.

Rnds 21-24: Knit around.

Rnd 25: Repeat Rnd 14: 30 sts.

Rnds 26 and 27: Knit around.

Rnd 28: Repeat Rnd 14: 24 sts.

Leaving sts on needles, lightly stuff Body.

Rnd 29: K2 tog around: 12 sts.

BACK NECK
Redistribute sts onto two needles, 6 sts each, with **wrong** side facing and working yarn on right hand end of one needle. Remove marker and begin working in rows.

Row 1: P1, purl increase 4 times *(Fig. 9, page 29)*, P1 across first needle **only**, leave remaining 6 sts on hold: 10 sts.

BODY
With Blue, cast 6 sts onto a double pointed needle; transfer 2 sts onto each of two other needles *(see Knitting in the Round, page 28)*.

Place a split ring marker around first cast on stitch to mark beginning of round *(see Markers, page 28)*. Begin working in rounds, making sure that first round is not twisted.

Rnd 1: Knit around.

Rnd 2: Knit increase in each st around *(Figs. 6a & b, page 29)*: 12 sts.

Rnds 3 and 4: Repeat Rnds 1 and 2: 24 sts.

Rnds 5 and 6: Knit around.

Rnd 7: (K1, knit increase) around: 36 sts.

Rnds 8-10: Knit around.

Rnd 11: (K2, knit increase) around: 48 sts.

Row 2: Slip 1 as if to **purl**, knit across.

Row 3: Slip 1 as if to **purl**, purl across.

Rows 4-12: Repeat Rows 2 and 3, 4 times; then repeat Row 2 once **more**.

HEAD
CROWN SHAPING

Row 1: Slip 1 as if to **purl**, P4, P2 tog *(Fig. 14, page 30)*, P1, leave remaining 2 sts unworked.

Row 2: Turn; slip 1 as if to **purl**, K1, K2 tog, K1, leave remaining 2 sts unworked.

Row 3: Turn; slip 1 as if to **purl**, P2, P2 tog, P1.

Row 4: K4, K2 tog, K1: 6 sts.

FACE

With same needle holding Crown sts, pick up 7 sts along first neck edge *(Fig. 16a, page 31)*. With an empty needle, knit across 6 front neck sts. With an empty needle, pick up 7 sts along second neck edge, then knit first 3 sts from first needle. Place split ring marker around first st to mark beginning of rnd. There will be 10 sts on first needle, 6 sts on second needle, and 10 sts on third needle, 26 sts total.

Rnd 1 (Decrease rnd): Knit across to last 3 sts on first needle, K2 tog, K1; knit across 6 sts on second needle; K1, SSK, knit across on third needle: 24 sts.

Rnd 2: Knit around.

Rnds 3-7: Repeat Rnds 1 and 2 twice, then repeat Rnd 1 once **more**: 18 sts.

Leaving sts on needles, lightly stuff Head.

Rnd 8: (SSK, K2, K2 tog) 3 times: 12 sts.

Rnd 9: Knit around.

Rnd 10: K2 tog around: 6 sts.

Lightly stuff Face.

Cut yarn, leaving a long end for sewing.

Thread yarn needle with long end and weave through remaining sts, pull **tightly** and secure end.

EAR (Make 2)
Ear is worked flat with two double pointed needles.

With Blue, cast on 4 sts.

Row 1: Knit increase in each st across: 8 sts.

Row 2: Purl across.

Row 3: (K1, knit increase) across: 12 sts.

Row 4: Purl across.

Row 5: K4, SSK, K2 tog, K4: 10 sts.

Row 6: Purl across.

Row 7: K3, SSK, K2 tog, K3: 8 sts.

Row 8: Purl across.

Row 9: SSK twice, K2 tog twice: 4 sts.

Row 10: P2 tog twice: 2 sts.

Bind off by passing the first st over the second st on the right needle, cut yarn and pull through last st leaving a long end for sewing.

TAIL
Tail is worked on two double pointed needles in I-cord rows.

With Blue, cast on 4 sts.

Rows 1-8: Slide sts to opposite end of needle, K4.

Row 9: Slide sts to opposite end of needle, K1, K2 tog, K1: 3 sts.

Instructions continued on page 12.

Rows 10-19: Slide sts to opposite end of needle, K3.

Row 20: Slide sts to opposite end of needle, K2 tog, K1: 2 sts.

Rows 21-34: Slide sts to opposite end of needle, K2.

Bind off by passing the first st over the second st on the right needle, cut yarn and pull through last st leaving a long end for sewing.

LEG (Make 4)

With Blue, cast 6 sts onto a double pointed needle; transfer 2 sts onto each of two other needles and place split ring marker around first st to mark beginning of rnd.

Rnds 1-18: Knit around.

FOOT

Rnd 1: K1, knit increase 4 times, K1: 10 sts.

Rnds 2-5: Knit around.

Rnd 6: K1, K2 tog 4 times, K1: 6 sts.

Rnd 7: Knit around.

Cut yarn, leaving a long end for sewing.

Stuff the Foot and the last 5 rnds of the Leg, leaving the rest of the Leg unstuffed.

Thread yarn needle with long end and weave through remaining sts, pull **tightly** and secure end.

FINISHING

Using photo as a guide for placement:
   Sew Legs to Body.
   Sew Tail to center back at base of Body.
   With purl side facing front, sew one Ear to each side of Head, beginning at top of Crown Shaping.
   With Yellow, work satin stitch for the nose **(Fig. 19, page 31)** and French knots for the eyes **(Fig. 18, page 31)**.
   Cut three, 8" (20.5 cm) pieces of Yellow yarn and thread through Face behind nose. Tie each side securely with an overhand knot. Trim for whiskers. ❖

blanket

 EASY

Finished Size: 36" (91.5 cm) square

MATERIALS
Bulky Weight Yarn
  (3 ounces, 135 yards
  (85 grams, 123 meters) per skein):
    6 skeins
40" (101.5 cm) Circular knitting needle,
  size 10 (6 mm) **or** size needed for gauge
Markers

GAUGE: In pattern,
          14 sts and 18 rows = 4" (10 cm)

BODY
Cast on 116 sts.

Row 1: Purl across.

Row 2 (Right side)**:** K2, ★ YO **(Fig. 17a, page 31)**, K2 tog **(Fig. 10, page 29)**, K4; repeat from ★ across.

Row 3: Purl across.

Row 4: Knit across.

Row 5: Purl across.

Row 6: K5, YO, K2 tog, ★ K4, YO, K2 tog; repeat from ★ across to last st, K1.

Row 7: Purl across.

Row 8: Knit across.

Rows 9-148: Repeat Rows 1-8, 17 times; then repeat Rows 1-4 once **more**.

Bind off all sts in **purl**.

EDGING
With **right** side facing, pick up 114 sts along first edge **(Figs. 16a & b, page 31)**, place marker **(see Markers, page 28)**, pick up a corner st, pick up 114 sts along next edge, place marker, pick up a corner st, pick up 114 sts along next edge, place marker, pick up a corner st, pick up 114 sts along last edge, place marker, pick up a corner st, place marker to mark beginning of rnd: 460 sts.

Rnd 1: M1L **(Figs. 7a & b, page 29)**, knit across to next marker, M1R **(Figs. 8a & b, page 29)**, slip marker, K1, ★ M1L, knit across to next marker, M1R, slip marker, K1; repeat from ★ around: 468 sts.

Rnd 2: Purl around.

Rnds 3-10: Repeat Rnds 1 and 2, 4 times.

Working same as Rnd 1, bind off all sts in **knit**. ❖

this little PIGGY

. . . .

oink
the
piggy

INTERMEDIATE

Finished Size: 6¹/₂" (16.5 cm) tall
(seated, excluding ears)

MATERIALS
Medium Weight Yarn
    Pink - 120 yards (110 meters)
    Black - small amount
Double pointed knitting needles, size 6 (4 mm)
    (set of 4) **or** size needed for gauge
Split ring marker
Polyester fiberfill
Yarn needle

GAUGE: In Stockinette Stitch.
    18 sts and 24 rows = 4" (10 cm)

Instructions begin on page 16.

Rnds 18-21: Knit around.

Rnds 22-32: Repeat Rnds 17-21 twice, then repeat Rnd 17 once **more**: 24 sts.

Leaving sts on the needles, lightly stuff Body.

Rnd 33: K2 tog around: 12 sts.

 **BACK NECK**

Redistribute sts onto two needles, 6 sts each, with **wrong** side facing and working yarn on right hand end of one needle. Remove marker and begin working in rows.

Row 1: Purl increase in each st across first needle only **(Fig. 9, page 29)**, leave remaining 6 sts on hold: 12 sts.

Row 2: Slip 1 as if to **purl**, knit across.

Row 3: Slip 1 as if to **purl**, purl across.

Rows 4-12: Repeat Rows 2 and 3, 4 times; then repeat Row 2 once **more**.

HEAD
CROWN SHAPING

Row 1: Slip 1 as if to **purl**, P5, P2 tog **(Fig. 14, page 30)**, P1, leave remaining 3 sts unworked.

 BODY

With Pink, cast 6 sts onto a double pointed needle; transfer 2 sts onto each of two other needles **(see Knitting in the Round, page 28)**.

Place a split ring marker around first cast on stitch to mark beginning of round **(see Markers, page 28)**. Begin working in rounds, making sure that first round is not twisted.

Rnd 1: Knit around.

Rnd 2: Knit increase in each st around **(Figs. 6a & b, page 29)**: 12 sts.

Rnds 3 and 4: Repeat Rnds 1 and 2: 24 sts.

Rnds 5 and 6: Knit around.

Rnd 7: (K1, knit increase) around: 36 sts.

Rnds 8-10: Knit around.

Rnd 11: (K2, knit increase) around: 48 sts.

Rnds 12-16: Knit around.

Rnd 17 (Decrease rnd)**:** ★ K2, SSK **(Figs. 11a-c, page 30)**, knit across to last 4 sts on needle, K2 tog **(Fig. 10, page 29)**, K2; repeat from ★ across each needle: 42 sts.

Row 2: Turn; slip 1 as if to **purl**, K1, K2 tog, K1, leave remaining 3 sts unworked.

Row 3: Turn; slip 1 as if to **purl**, P2, P2 tog, P1, leave last st unworked.

Row 4: Turn; slip 1 as if to **purl**, K3, K2 tog, K1, leave last st unworked.

Row 5: Turn; slip 1 as if to **purl**, P4, P2 tog.

Row 6: Turn; K5, K2 tog: 6 sts.

FACE
With same needle holding Crown sts, pick up 7 sts along first neck edge **(Fig. 16a, page 31)**. With an empty needle, knit across 6 front neck sts. With an empty needle, pick up 7 sts along second neck edge, then knit first 3 sts from first needle. Place split ring marker around first st to mark beginning of rnd. There will be 10 sts on first needle, 6 sts on second needle, and 10 sts on third needle, 26 sts total.

Rnd 1: Knit around.

Rnd 2 (Decrease rnd)**:** Knit across to last 3 sts on first needle, K2 tog, K1; knit across 6 sts on second needle; K1, SSK, knit across on third needle: 24 sts.

Rnds 3-9: Repeat Rnds 1 and 2, 3 times; then repeat Rnd 1 once **more**: 18 sts. Leaving sts on needles, lightly stuff Head.

Rnd 10: K2 tog around: 9 sts.

Cut yarn, leaving a long end for sewing.

Thread yarn needle with long end and weave through remaining sts, pull **tightly** and secure end.

 SNOUT
With Pink, cast 6 sts onto a double pointed needle; transfer 2 sts onto each of two other needles. Place split ring marker around first st to mark beginning of rnd.

Rnd 1: Knit increase in each st around: 12 sts.

Rnd 2: Knit around.

Bind off all sts in **knit**; leave last st on right needle, do **not** cut yarn.

With **purl** side facing, skip first st and pick up one st in each st around **(Fig. 16b, page 31)**, picking up 4 sts with each of three needles: 12 sts.

Last Rnd: Knit around.

Bind off all sts in **knit**.

 EAR (Make 2)
Ear is worked flat with two double pointed needles.

With Pink, cast on 9 sts.

Row 1: Purl across.

Row 2: K2, SSK, K1, K2 tog, K2: 7 sts.

Row 3: Purl across.

Row 4: K1, SSK, K1, K2 tog, K1: 5 sts.

Row 5: Purl across.

Row 6: SSK, K1, K2 tog: 3 sts.

Row 7: Purl across.

Row 8: K1, K2 tog: 2 sts.

Bind off by passing the first st over the second st on the right needle, cut yarn and pull through last st leaving a long end for sewing.

 TAIL
Tail is worked flat with two double pointed needles.

With Pink, cast on 10 sts.

Row 1: Knit increase in each st across: 20 sts.

Bind off all sts in **knit**.

Instructions continued on page 18.

LEG (Make 4)

With Pink, cast 12 sts onto a double pointed needle; transfer 4 sts onto each of two other needles. Place split ring marker around first st to mark beginning of rnd.

Rnds 1-15: Knit around.

FOOT

Rnd 1: K3, knit increase 6 times, K3: 18 sts.

Rnds 2-5: Knit around.

Rnd 6: K3, K2 tog 6 times, K3: 12 sts.

Rnd 7: Knit around.

Rnd 8: K2 tog around: 6 sts.

Cut yarn, leaving a long end for sewing.

Stuff the Foot and the last 5 rnds of the Leg, leaving the rest of the Leg unstuffed.

Thread yarn needle with long end and weave through remaining sts, pull **tightly** and secure end.

 FINISHING

Using photo as a guide for placement:
  Sew Legs to Body.
  Stuff Snout and sew to center of Face.
  Fold Ear at center st, then sew to Head with purl side facing front at first and last cast on sts. Thread yarn needle with long end. Insert needle through center st on Row 4, then through center st at cast on and into Head. Pull up to partially fold in the tip of the Ear. Secure ends.
  With Black, work French knots for the eyes above the Snout, even with each Ear *(Fig. 18, page 31)*.
  Sew Tail to back at base of Body. ❖

 blanket

  ◼◼◻◻ EASY

 Finished Size: 30" x 40" (76 cm x 101.5 cm)

 MATERIALS

Medium Weight Yarn ◀4▶
  (7 ounces, 355 yards
  (200 grams, 325 meters) per skein**)**:
    Peach - 2 skeins
    Pink - 1 skein
40" (101.5 cm) Circular knitting needle, size 10
  (6 mm) **or** size needed for gauge
Markers

GAUGE: In pattern,
  15 sts and 21 rows = 4" (10 cm)

STRIPE SEQUENCE

72 Rows Pink, 2 rows Peach,
8 rows Pink, 4 rows Peach, 6 rows
Pink, 6 rows Peach, 4 rows Pink,
8 rows Peach, 2 rows Pink,
72 rows Peach.

BODY

With Pink, cast on 95 sts.

Row 1: Purl across.

Row 2 (Right side): K1, (WYF slip 1
as if to **purl**, K1) across.

Row 3: Purl across.

Row 4: K2, WYF slip 1 as if to **purl**,
(K1, WYF slip 1 as if to **purl**) across
to last 2 sts, K2.

Rows 5-184: Following Stripe
Sequence above, repeat
Rows 1-4, 45 times.

Bind off all sts in **purl**.

RUFFLE

With **right** side facing and
Peach, pick up 138 sts along
first long edge *(Figs. 16a & b,
page 31)*, place marker *(see
Markers, page 28)*, pick up a
corner st, pick up 93 sts along
cast on edge, place marker,
pick up a corner st, pick up
138 sts along second long edge,
place marker, pick up a corner
st, pick up 93 sts along bind off
row, place marker, pick up a
corner st, place marker to mark
beginning of rnd: 466 sts.

Rnd 1: ★ Knit increase in each st across to next marker
(Figs. 6a & b, page 29), slip marker, K1; repeat from ★
around: 928 sts.

Rnd 2: M1L *(Figs. 7a & b, page 29)*, knit across to next
marker, M1R *(Figs. 8a & b, page 29)*, slip marker, K1,
★ M1L, knit across to next marker, M1R, slip marker, K1;
repeat from ★ around: 936 sts.

Rnd 3: Knit around.

Rnds 4-10: Repeat Rnds 2 and 3, 3 times; then repeat
Rnd 2 once **more**.

Rnd 11: Purl around.

Working same as Rnd 2, bind off all sts in **knit**. ❖

duck, duck GOOSE

• •

quack the duck

INTERMEDIATE

Finished Size: 6" (15 cm) tall
(seated, excluding Head knot)

MATERIALS
Medium Weight Yarn **MEDIUM 4**
   Yellow - 80 yards (73 meters)
   Orange - 15 yards (13.5 meters)
   Black - small amount
   White novelty yarn - small amount
Double pointed knitting needles, size 6 (4 mm)
   (set of 4) **or** size needed for gauge
Small stitch holder - 2
Split ring marker
Polyester fiberfill
Yarn needle

GAUGE: In Stockinette Stitch,
   18 sts and 24 rows = 4" (10 cm)

Instructions begin on page 22.

 **BOTTOM**

With Yellow, cast 6 sts onto a double pointed needle; transfer 2 sts onto each of two other needles *(see Knitting in the Round, page 28)*.

Place a split ring marker around first cast on stitch to mark beginning of round *(see Markers, page 28)*. Begin working in rounds, making sure that first round is not twisted.

Rnd 1: Knit around.

Rnd 2: Knit increase in each st around *(Figs. 6a & b, page 29)*: 12 sts.

Rnds 3 and 4: Repeat Rnds 1 and 2: 24 sts.

Rnds 5 and 6: Knit around.

Rnd 7: (K1, knit increase) around: 36 sts.

Rnds 8-10: Knit around.

Rnd 11: (K2, knit increase) around: 48 sts.

TAIL SHAPING

Slip last 8 sts on first needle onto a stitch holder, then slip first 8 sts on third needle onto a second stitch holder *(Fig. 2)*. Remove marker.

Fig. 2

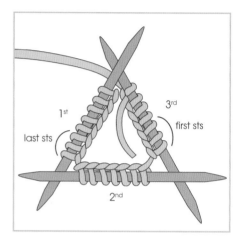

Using the third needle, knit remaining 8 sts on the first needle: 16 sts.

Begin working in rows.

Row 1: P9, P2 tog *(Fig. 14, page 30)*, P1, leave remaining 4 sts unworked.

Row 2: Turn; slip 1 as if to **purl**, K3, SSK *(Figs. 11a-c, page 30)*, K1, leave remaining 4 sts unworked.

Row 3: Turn; slip 1 as if to **purl**, P4, P2 tog, P1, leave remaining 2 sts unworked.

Row 4: Turn; slip 1 as if to **purl**, K5, SSK, K1, leave remaining 2 sts unworked.

Row 5: Turn; slip 1 as if to **purl**, P6, P2 tog, P1.

Row 6: K8, K2 tog **(Fig. 10, page 29)**, K1: 10 sts.

BODY

Slip 8 sts from second stitch holder onto an empty needle, then slip first 5 sts from working needle onto opposite end of same needle.

Begin working in rounds.

Rnd 1: Continuing with same needle, K8 from first stitch holder, K 16 across second needle, K 13 across third needle, place marker to mark beginning of rnd: 42 sts.

Rnd 2: Knit increase, knit around to last st, knit increase: 44 sts.

Rnd 3: Knit around.

Rnds 4-7: Repeat Rnds 2 and 3 twice: 48 sts.

Rnd 8 (Decrease rnd): ★ K2, SSK, knit across to last 4 sts on needle, K2 tog, K2; repeat from ★ across each needle: 42 sts.

Rnds 9-13: Knit around.

Rnds 14-20: Repeat Rnds 8-13 once, then repeat Rnd 8 once **more**: 30 sts.

Rnds 21-23: Knit around.

Rnd 24: Repeat Rnd 8: 24 sts.

Leaving sts on needles, lightly stuff Body.

Rnd 25: K2 tog around: 12 sts.

BACK NECK

Slip last st from first needle onto second needle, then slip first st from third needle onto opposite end of same needle **(Fig. 3)**. With third needle, knit remaining 3 sts on first needle: 6 sts on each needle. Remove marker and begin working in rows.

Fig. 3

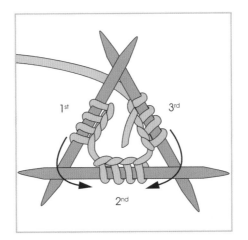

Row 1: Purl increase in each st across first needle **only (Fig. 9, page 29)**, leave remaining 6 sts on hold: 12 sts.

Row 2: Slip 1 as if to **purl**, knit across.

Row 3: Slip 1 as if to **purl**, purl across.

Rows 4-12: Repeat Rows 2 and 3, 4 times; then repeat Row 2 once **more**.

HEAD
CROWN SHAPING

Row 1: Slip 1 as if to **purl**, P6, P2 tog, P1, leave remaining 2 sts unworked.

Row 2: Turn; slip 1 as if to **purl**, K3, K2 tog, K1, leave remaining 2 sts unworked.

Row 3: Turn; slip 1 as if to **purl**, P4, P2 tog, P1.

Row 4: Slip 1 as if to **purl**, K5, K2 tog, K1: 8 sts.

Row 5: Slip 1 as if to **purl**, P5, P2 tog: 7 sts.

Row 6: K5, K2 tog: 6 sts.

Instructions continued on page 24.

FACE

With same needle holding Crown sts, pick up 8 sts along first neck edge *(Fig. 16a, page 31)*. With an empty needle, knit across 6 front neck sts. With an empty needle, pick up 8 sts along second neck edge, then knit first 3 sts from first needle. Place split ring marker around first st to mark beginning of rnd. There will be 11 sts on first needle, 6 sts on second needle, 11 sts on third needle, 28 sts total.

Rnd 1: K5, K2 tog 3 times, K6, K2 tog 3 times, K5: 22 sts.

Rnd 2: Knit around.

Rnd 3: K5, K2 tog, K8, SSK, K5: 20 sts.

Rnd 4: K1, SSK, K4, SSK, K2, K2 tog, K4, K2 tog, K1: 16 sts.

Rnd 5: K2 tog 3 times, K4, K2 tog 3 times: 10 sts.

Rnd 6: K1, K2 tog, K4, SSK, K1: 8 sts.

Bind off all sts in **knit**.

Cut yarn leaving a long end for sewing. Stuff Head.

Matching sts, sew Face seam.

BEAK (Make 2)

Beak is worked flat with two double pointed needles.

With Orange, cast on 4 sts.

Row 1: Knit across.

Row 2: Knit increase in each st across: 8 sts.

Row 3: Knit across.

Row 4: (K1, knit increase) across: 12 sts.

Rows 5-8: Knit across.

Row 9: K4, SSK, K2 tog, K4: 10 sts.

Row 10: Knit across.

Row 11: K3, SSK, K2 tog, K3: 8 sts.

Bind off all sts in **knit**.

WING (Make 2)

Wing is worked flat with two double pointed needles.

With Yellow, cast on 8 sts.

Row 1: Knit across.

Row 2: Knit increase 5 times, K3: 13 sts.

Row 3: Knit across.

Row 4: K 10, slip 1 as if to **purl**, bring yarn to **front**, slip st back onto left needle, leave remaining sts unworked.

Row 5: Turn; K 10.

Row 6: K9, slip 1 as if to **purl**, bring yarn to **front**, slip st back onto left needle, leave remaining sts unworked.

Row 7: Turn; K9.

Row 8: K8, slip 1 as if to **purl**, bring yarn to **front**, slip st back onto left needle, leave remaining sts unworked.

Row 9: Turn; K8.

Row 10: K7, slip 1 as if to **purl**, bring yarn to **front**, slip st back onto left needle, leave remaining sts unworked.

Row 11: Turn; K7.

Row 12: K6, slip 1 as if to **purl**, bring yarn to **front**, slip st back onto left needle, leave remaining sts unworked.

Row 13: Turn; K6.

Row 14: K5, slip 1 as if to **purl**, bring yarn to **front**, slip st back onto left needle, leave remaining sts unworked.

Row 15: Turn; K5.

Row 16: K4, slip 1 as if to **purl**, bring yarn to **front**, slip st back onto left needle, leave remaining sts unworked.

Row 17: Turn; K4.

Row 18: K3, slip 1 as if to **purl**, bring yarn to **front**, slip st back onto left needle, leave remaining sts unworked.

Row 19: Turn; K3.

Row 20: K2, slip 1 as if to **purl**, bring yarn to **front**, slip st back onto left needle, leave remaining sts unworked.

Row 21: Turn; K2.

Row 22: K1, slip 1 as if to **purl**, bring yarn to **front**, slip st back onto left needle, leave remaining sts unworked.

Row 23: Turn; K1.

K2 tog to form wing tip, then bind off all sts in **knit**, leaving wraps unworked.

FOOT (Make 2)
Foot is worked flat with two double pointed needles.

With Orange, cast on 17 sts.

Row 1: K8, P1, K8.

Row 2 (Right side)**:** K7, (slip 2, K1, P2SSO *(Figs. 13a & b, page 30))*, K7: 15 sts.

Row 3: K7, P1, K7.

Row 4: K6, slip 2, K1, P2SSO, K6: 13 sts.

Row 5: K6, P1, K6.

Row 6: K5, slip 2, K1, P2SSO, K5: 11 sts.

Row 7: K5, P1, K5.

Row 8: K4, slip 2, K1, P2SSO, K4: 9 sts.

Row 9: K4, P1, K4.

Row 10: K3, slip 2, K1, P2SSO, K3: 7 sts.

Row 11: K3, P1, K3.

Row 12: K2, slip 2, K1, P2SSO, K2: 5 sts.

LEG
Begin working in I-cord rows.

Rows 1-15: Slide sts to opposite end of needle, K5.

Bind off all sts in **knit**.

FINISHING
Using photo as a guide for placement:
   Sew cast on edge of each Wing to side of Body with bound off edge at top.
   Sew each Leg to Body.
   Sew each Beak half to Face at seam; then sew sides of Beak together.
   With Black, work French knots for the eyes *(Fig. 18, page 31)*.
   Cut two short lengths of white novelty yarn, fold in half, and attach to Head as a fringe *(Figs. 1a & b, page 7)*; trim. ❖

blanket

Finished Size: 37^1/$_2$" (95.5 cm) square

MATERIALS

Medium Weight Yarn **4**
 (3^1/$_2$ ounces, 200 yards
 (100 grams, 183 meters) per skein)**:**
  White - 8 skeins
  Yellow - 1 skein
40" (101.5 cm) Circular knitting needles,
 size 13 (9 mm) **or** size needed for gauge
Crochet hook, size N (9 mm) (for Edging)

Blanket is worked holding two strands of yarn
together throughout.

GAUGE: In pattern, with two strands of
 yarn held together,
 12 sts = 4" (10 cm)

BODY

With two strands of White, cast on 112 sts.

Row 1 (Right side)**:** Purl across.

Row 2: ★ (K1, P1, K1) **all** in same st, P3 tog
(Fig. 15, page 30); repeat from ★ across.

Row 3: Purl across.

Row 4: ★ P3 tog, (K1, P1, K1) **all** in same st;
repeat from ★ across.

Repeat Rows 1-4 for pattern until Body
measures approximately 37" (94 cm) from
cast on edge, ending by working a **wrong**
side row.

Bind off all sts in **purl**.

EDGING
See Crochet Stitches, page 32.

With **right** side facing, join two strands of
Yellow with slip st in any corner st, ch 1; (sc,
ch 4, sc) in same st, ch 1, ★ skip next st,
(sc, ch 4, sc) in next st, ch 1; repeat from ★
around; join with slip st to first sc, finish off. ❖

ABBREVIATIONS

ch(s)	chain(s)
cm	centimeters
K	knit
M1L	make one left
M1R	make one right
mm	millimeters
P	purl
PSSO	pass slipped stitch over
P2SSO	pass 2 slipped stitches over
Rnd(s)	Round(s)
sc	single crochet(s)
SSK	slip, slip, knit
st(s)	stitch(es)
tog	together
WYF	with yarn in front
YO	yarn over

★ — work instructions following ★ as many **more** times as indicated in addition to the first time.

( ) or [ ] — work enclosed instructions **as many** times as specified by the number immediately following **or** work all enclosed instructions in the stitch indicated **or** contains explanatory remarks.

colon (:) — the number(s) given after a colon at the end of a row or round denote(s) the number of stitches you should have on that row or round.

	LACE 0	SUPER FINE 1	FINE 2	LIGHT 3	MEDIUM 4	BULKY 5	SUPER BULKY 6
Yarn Weight Symbol & Names							
Type of Yarns in Category	Fingering, size 10 crochet thread	Sock, Fingering, Baby	Sport, Baby	DK, Light Worsted	Worsted, Afghan, Aran	Chunky, Craft, Rug	Bulky, Roving
Knit Gauge Range* in Stockinette St to 4" (10 cm)	33-40** sts	27-32 sts	23-26 sts	21-24 sts	16-20 sts	12-15 sts	6-11 sts
Advised Needle Size Range	000-1	1 to 3	3 to 5	5 to 7	7 to 9	9 to 11	11 and larger

KNIT TERMINOLOGY

UNITED STATES	INTERNATIONAL
gauge =	tension
bind off =	cast off
yarn over (YO) =	yarn forward (yfwd) **or** yarn around needle (yrn)

*GUIDELINES ONLY: The chart above reflects the most commonly used gauges and needle sizes for specific yarn categories.

** Lace weight yarns are usually knitted on larger needles to create lacy openwork patterns. Accordingly, a gauge range is difficult to determine. Always follow the gauge stated in your pattern.

KNITTING NEEDLES															
U.S.	0	1	2	3	4	5	6	7	8	9	10	10½	11	13	15	17
U.K.	13	12	11	10	9	8	7	6	5	4	3	2	1	00	000	---
Metric - mm	2	2.25	2.75	3.25	3.5	3.75	4	4.5	5	5.5	6	6.5	8	9	10	12.75

BEGINNER	Projects for first-time knitters using basic knit and purl stitches. Minimal shaping.
EASY	Projects using basic stitches, repetitive stitch patterns, simple color changes, and simple shaping and finishing.
INTERMEDIATE	Projects with a variety of stitches, such as basic cables and lace, simple intarsia, double-pointed needles and knitting in the round needle techniques, mid-level shaping and finishing.
EXPERIENCED	Projects using advanced techniques and stitches, such as short rows, fair isle, more intricate intarsia, cables, lace patterns, and numerous color changes.

GAUGE

Exact gauge is **essential** for proper size. Before beginning your project, make a sample swatch in the yarn and needle specified. After completing the swatch, measure it, counting your stitches and rows carefully. If your swatch is larger or smaller than specified, **make another, changing needle size to get the correct gauge.** Keep trying until you find the size needles that will give you the specified gauge.

 ## KNITTING IN THE ROUND

When working on a project that is too small to use circular needles, double pointed needles are required. Divide the stitches into thirds and slip ⅓ of the stitches onto each of the double pointed needles *(Fig. 4)*, forming a triangle and leaving the last needle of the set empty. With the last needle, knit across the first needle *(Fig. 5)*. You will now have an empty needle with which to knit the stitches from the next needle. Work the first stitch on each needle firmly to prevent gaps.

 # MARKERS

As a convenience to you, we have used markers to help distinguish the beginning of a pattern or a round. Place markers as instructed. When using double pointed needles and marking the beginning of a round, a split ring marker is placed around the first stitch to prevent the marker from slipping off the needle. When you reach the marker, move it to the new stitch after it is made. When using circular needles, you may use markers or tie a length of contrasting color yarn around the needle. When you reach a marker on each round, slip it from the left needle to the right needle; remove it when instructed or when no longer needed.

Fig. 4

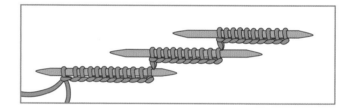

Fig. 5

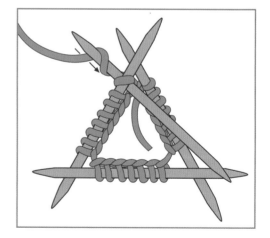

🧶 INCREASES
KNIT INCREASE

Knit the next stitch but do **not** slip the old stitch off the left needle *(Fig. 6a)*. Insert the right needle into the **back** loop of the **same** stitch and knit it *(Fig. 6b)*, then slip the old stitch off the left needle.

MAKE ONE LEFT *(abbreviated M1L)*

Insert the **left** needle under the horizontal strand between the stitches from **front** to **back** *(Fig. 7a)*. Then knit into the **back** of the strand *(Fig. 7b)*.

MAKE ONE RIGHT
   (abbreviated M1R)

Insert the **left** needle under the horizontal strand between the stitches from **back** to **front** *(Fig. 8a)*. Then knit into the **front** of the strand *(Fig. 8b)*.

PURL INCREASE

Purl the next stitch but do **not** slip the old stitch off the left needle. Insert the right needle into the **back** loop of the **same** stitch from **back** to **front** *(Fig. 9)* and purl it. Slip the old stitch off the left needle.

🧶 DECREASES
KNIT 2 TOGETHER
   (abbreviated K2 tog)

Insert the right needle into the **front** of the first two stitches on the left needle as if to **knit** *(Fig. 10)*, then **knit** them together as if they were one stitch.

Fig. 6a
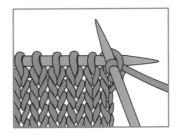

Fig. 6b
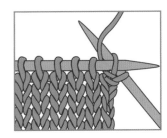

Fig. 7a
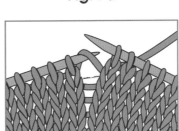

Fig. 7b
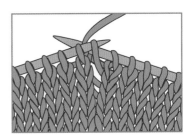

Fig. 8a
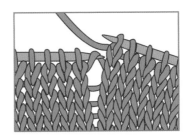

Fig. 8b
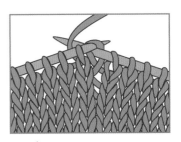

Fig. 9
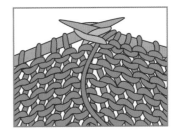

Fig. 10
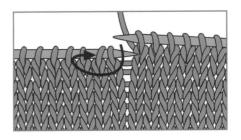

SLIP, SLIP, KNIT (abbreviated SSK)

Separately slip two stitches as if to **knit** (*Fig. 11a*). Insert the left needle into the **front** of both slipped stitches (*Fig. 11b*) and knit them together as if they were one stitch (*Fig. 11c*).

Fig. 11a

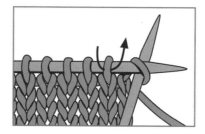

Fig. 11b

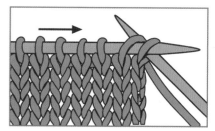

SLIP 1, KNIT 2, PASS SLIPPED STITCH OVER
(abbreviated slip 1, K2, PSSO)

Slip one stitch as if to **knit**. Knit the next two stitches. With the left needle, bring the slipped stitch over the two knit stitches (*Fig. 12*) and off the needle.

Fig. 11c

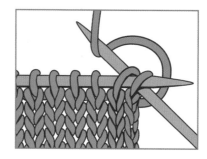

Fig. 12

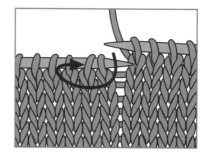

SLIP 2, KNIT 1, PASS 2 SLIPPED STITCHES OVER
(abbreviated slip 2, K1, P2SSO)

With yarn in back, slip two stitches together as if to **knit** (*Fig. 13a*), then knit the next stitch. With the left needle, bring both slipped stitches over the knit stitch (*Fig. 13b*) and off the needle.

Fig. 13a

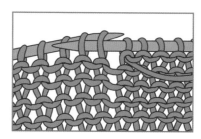

Fig. 13b

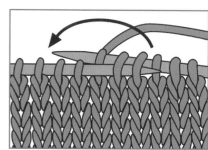

PURL 2 TOGETHER
(abbreviated P2 tog)

Insert the right needle into the **front** of the first two stitches on the left needle as if to **purl** (*Fig. 14*), then **purl** them together as if they were one stitch.

Fig. 14

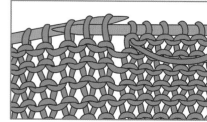

Fig. 15

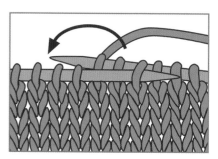

PURL 3 TOGETHER
(abbreviated P3 tog)

Insert the right needle into the **front** of the first three stitches on the left needle as if to **purl** (*Fig. 15*), then **purl** them together as if they were one stitch.

PICKING UP STITCHES

When instructed to pick up stitches, insert the needle from the **front** to the **back** under two strands at the edge of the worked piece *(Figs. 16a & b)*. Put the yarn around the needle as if to **knit**, then bring the needle with the yarn back through the stitch to the right side, resulting in a stitch on the needle. Repeat this along the edge, picking up the required number of stitches. A crochet hook may be helpful to pull yarn through.

Fig. 16a

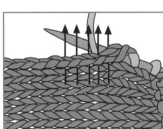

Fig. 16b

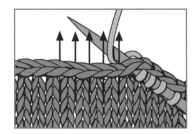

YARN OVER *(abbreviated YO)*

after a knit, before a knit

Bring the yarn forward **between** the needles, then back **over** the top of the right hand needle, so that it is now in position to knit the next stitch *(Fig. 17a)*.

after a purl, before a purl

Take yarn over the right hand needle to the **back**, then forward **under** it, so that it is now in position to purl the next stitch *(Fig. 17b)*.

Fig. 17a

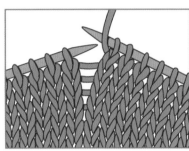

Fig. 17b

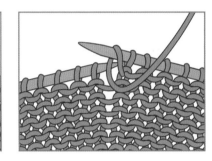

EMBROIDERY STITCHES
FRENCH KNOT

Bring needle up at 1. Wrap yarn around the needle the desired number of times and insert needle at 2, holding end of yarn with non-stitching fingers *(Fig. 18)*. Tighten knot; then pull needle through, holding yarn until it must be released.

Fig. 18

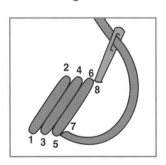

SATIN STITCH

Satin stitch is a series of straight stitches worked side by side so they touch but do not overlap. Come up at odd numbers and go down at even numbers *(Fig. 19)*.

Fig. 19

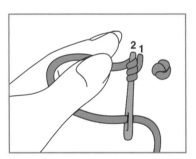

BASIC CROCHET STITCHES

CHAIN (abbreviated ch)

To work a chain stitch, bring the yarn **over** hook from back to front, catching the yarn with the hook and turning the hook slightly toward you to keep the yarn from slipping off. Draw the yarn through the loop on the hook (*Fig. 20*).

Fig. 20

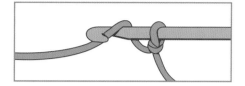

SLIP STITCH (abbreviated slip st)

To work a slip stitch, insert hook in stitch indicated, YO and draw through st and through loop on hook (*Fig. 21*).

Fig. 21

SINGLE CROCHET (abbreviated sc)

Insert hook in stitch indicated, YO and pull up a loop, YO and draw through both loops on hook (*Fig. 22*).

Fig. 22

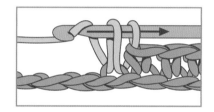